2017 2fast2house / oh! map books
http://2fast2house.com
2fast2house@gmail.com

ISBN 978-0-9978759-3-5

photos on pages 8, 11 and 41, drawing on page 51 and some text on page 44 by irene milsom. all other text and images by moss angel witchmonstr except where noted.

excerpts were originally published in Witch Craft Mag, Black Warrior Review, Gulf Coast, Puerto del Sol, The Wanderer, Pinwheel, Curious Specimens Anthology, Spy Kids Review & TRNSFR.

design by moss angel witchmonstr.

SEA-WITCH
by moss angel witchmonstr
volume one: may she lay us waste

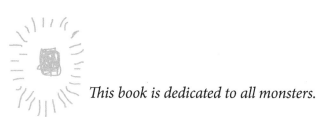 *This book is dedicated to all monsters.*

Fuck the police.

~gay~

CAST OF CHARACTERS

Narrator (Sara) – Gosh, where to start? Only one of many Saras. Telling this story. She/her or they/them pronouns.

Sea-Witch – A glittering cascade of water that froze in place to be lived in but accidentally ended up capable of true emotion. Precious & needs to be held. Gets cold like all living creatures. ETC ETC You get the idea. She/her.

Meteor (may she lay us waste) – Far away. Loves Girls With Assholes. Flat affect. Probably going to kill us all one day. She/her.

dog that showed up to hang out with sea-witch – Really fun & cute. Didn't mention their pronouns.

78 Men Who Cause Pain (aka 78MWCP) – I hate these guys. Just the worst. Go around being nice to each other so they can pretend they aren't literally hurting every other thing that exists. He/him.

small animals who hid their faces from the sun – Only exist in Sara's dream. Didn't ask what kind of animals? Maybe people. They/them?

People – Don't exist???? Secretly monsters??? They/them.

Dog-Witch – THE BEST!!!! Pretty much made everything. Helped a lot of people. Probably not perfect but honestly like, who cares ze is so nice & great? Ze/hir pronouns.

airless faces – Any thing that lived in the water before Dog-Witch made land. Not really a useful term anymore. It/its.

Air-Witch – Lived with rats. Ate dirt. Dies kind of a lot of times? She/her.

Water-Witch – idk???

Dirt-Witch – Beautiful & loves horses. She/her.

Milk-Witch – Round & does a lot of warm dialing. All those little number buttons in the mouths of infants. She/her.

Deeps-Witch – idk??

Old-Seagull-Witch – Works at University of Crater. Has a girlfriend & they do sex stuff. She/her.

Strawberry-Witch – Super cute. Keeps her seeds on the outside. Tried camming for awhile but wasn't very good at it. Has creepy dreams. Last I heard she bought a van & was living in it. She/her.

Leg-Witch – Literally another witch's leg. One of Dog-Witch's sisters. Doesn't talk much. She/her.

Candle-Witch – idk??

Less-Held-Witch – Learned about ghosts. Super crushing on Glass-Witch. She/her.

Moss-Witch – idk...

Dead-Jellyfish-Witch – *shrugs*

Stone-Witch – Totally hooked up with Dog-Witch. Also her own full being who lived a full life & had her own experiences thank you very much. She/her.

Wood-Witch – idk!!!

Glass-Witch – Super cool & cute. Likes Less-Held-Witch. But how much? She/her pronouns.

Airless-Face-Witch - Twin of God-Witch. She/her.

God-Witch – Twin of Airless-Face-Witch. She/her.

Death-Witch – God dammit. Fucking fuck. I'm so sorry. She/her.

ha-ha-ha (or ah-ah-ah) – Very mysterious. Unknown? Doesn't exists? Barely does? Loves cucumbers. ???? pronouns??

Bears – Mean. Used to do a lot of bad-guy things. Eat berries & nuts. They/them.

Lava – Hates bears, who kept it prisoner. Loves Dog-Witch. Likes helping with formation of monsters. It/Its

Girl who tried to cool with her mouth the lava around another girl – Possibly could have changed relationships in the world from being about power to being about care. Unfortunately, isn't real. She/her.

Infants - Sad? Love Milk-Witch. One of them works in a gift shop. They/them? Probably ask each one.

A Pit Filled 15 Feet Deep With Rotting Dresses - Just shows up one day? Idk. Ze/hir.

Girls With Assholes - Cool band. Nobody knows who the members are. They/them.

University of Crater - Place where people research pain. Honestly, probably funded by the 78 men. It/its.

The Living Creatures - Live in the woods or something. Idk. It/its.

minor god of pain - Honestly probably fake. Probably just one of the 78 men being an asshole. They/them.

boys - not real. they/them.

Angels - More like gayngels. it/its.

deadname - Weird one?! Hangs out with Strawberry-Witch and/or Sara. Smells like rainwater. xe/xym/xyr.

gaygod11.png - Literally a file on a computer? Digital. It/its.

Real Living Creature Whom Sea-Witch Kissed After Her Birth - Never knows what time it is. Actually rly beautiful singing voice. She/Her or It/its.

when they come 4 us
we will climb the trees

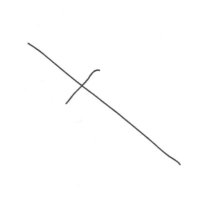

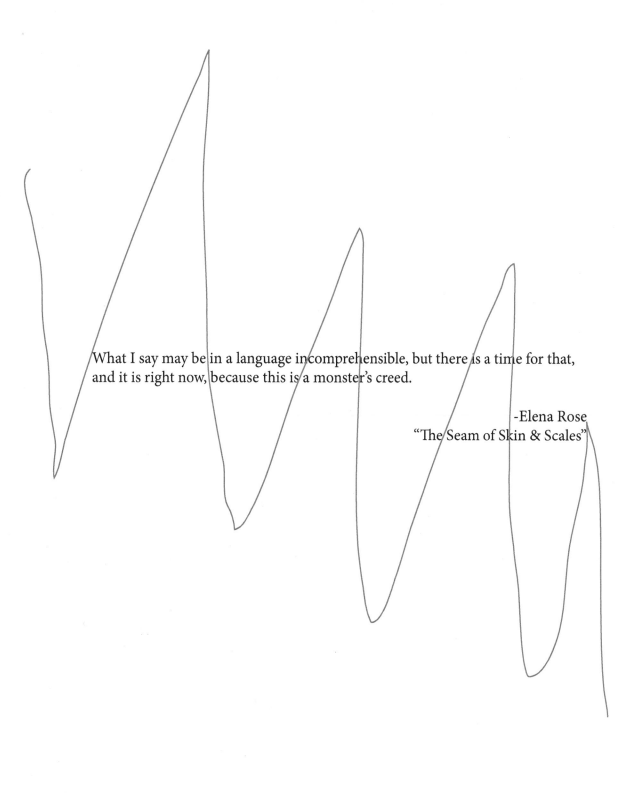

What I say may be in a language incomprehensible, but there is a time for that, and it is right now, because this is a monster's creed.

-Elena Rose
"The Seam of Skin & Scales"

TRANS MEMOIR 1

I am not here to talk about my body. The reason I am writing this is to keep a record of Sea-Witch & the events that happened regarding her. I wish I had another way to tell this, but for now I will speak of the events & occasionally will do so through my body, though I want you to understand that my body is not the focus. My body is not available for consumption. There might be times when I make it appear to be available for consumption & there might be times I want to be consumed, but I want to be clear about this. My body is not available.

I was created when my skin shed its mother. This is one of the ways I was formed. Formation, in the Sea-Witchean sense, happens within "systems". It has a specific smell. The systems of formation are many, some involve lava. Mine, in particular, involved a great deal of lava, which cooled into rock over the course of years. Formation, for most, takes many years. Generations of my family were formed first in Sea-Witch, as was I, but the people whose bodies created mine have never seen Sea-Witch & most likely doubt her existence.

SEA-WITCH 1 & 2

When I was living in Sea-Witch the sand held me on bright mornings. Small walls of it pressed on my sides & back & I pressed small walls of it in return with each breath. Species unfamiliar with Sea-Witch should know three things about her:

1. She is a monster & this would always be the case in a world that had created the idea of monsters to use to describe things like her.
2. She cries at television shows about other monsters.
3. Long periods of time can pass when no one tells you you are worthwhile & long periods of time can pass when you don't understand the words of those who are telling you. It is difficult to know the difference.

When I was living in Sea-Witch I was also a monster. When I was living in Sea-Witch I saw a television show about a little girl who put her dolls in a duffle bag with two sandwiches In Case Of An Emergency. Her mother worried about her when she found the bag, because she knew her daughter would someday run away. This was not what the girl pictured when she made the bag but it was what she ended up using it for. The mother did not confront her daughter about it because she knew her daughter was a monster & she knew that real monsters have no mothers. When I was living in Sea-Witch I got this television show tattooed on my arms & hands because it explained my life to others who wondered why I would live in a place like Sea-Witch.

When I was living in Sea-Witch sleep came when it did & disappeared later & hunger was similar. There is no cause & effect in Sea-Witch & everything happens at once. I was born in Sea-Witch even though I wasn't & I am still in Sea-Witch even though I am not.

When I was living in Sea-Witch people murdered her every day. Monsters exist to be slain, which is a word for murder that is mostly used for monsters. When I was living in Sea-Witch I had more friends, all of whom lived in Sea-Witches of their own. Crying is a kind of involuntary prayer we have in Sea-Witch where sea comes from your eyes, which is the place you receive light in order to understand it. When I was living in Sea-Witch I never understood light & I still don't. This hasn't changed about me.

When I was living in Sea-Witch I wrote a poem that everyone in Sea-Witch loved. I won't tell you which one because it doesn't matter which one. Think of any one of them & that is the one. When I was living in Sea-Witch I put a sign above the entrance that said There Is a Dead Thing Between My Legs & I Am Naming Myself Sara. I spent the rest of the day pushing crows underwater.

You do not get to come to Sea-Witch. I will never let you in.

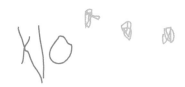

6

In Sea-Witch all day I go to church. I am always in church there & the church is where we sing songs to a meteor we hope will fall on us. If you understand Sea-Witch it will be clear why this religion is so popular.

In Sea-Witch we pray that we will not be murdered while at the same time we pray for death. It is a specific kind of prayer that you can only make when the lights are off, but you can sing the songs, you can't help singing them, in your head all day as you buy fabric. In Sea-Witch we buy so much fabric to drape over everything in our rooms. The smoke sticks in it & our arms hang limp. In Sea-Witch I sewed the word dying on my couch in Sea-Witch I was very melodramatic like this before I died. It is all over Sea-Witch now how I did this. How I died there & was melodramatic before I died.

In Sea-Witch the meteor came,
In Sea-Witch we were lost,
In Sea-Witch we drew circles with our eyes on the ceilings that will always be there.

I, a girl, married a girl in Sea-Witch & the priestess pronounced us wives there & prayed again for the meteor to come smash us all along the rocks there on the river-beach.

Before I lived in Sea-Witch I was in love with Sea-Witch & daydreamed about stroking her hair & pushing my mouth into hers & about hers pushing back. I would wake at night & find myself thinking about gentle falling asleep with her legs between mine, her soft clit by my clit. Before I lived in Sea-Witch I was in love with Sea-Witch & this love was a physical thing I carried in my arms but hid. Before I lived in Sea-Witch I called the feeling of love "Sea-Witch" & I called myself danger & sadness, mountain & sand.

Sea-Witch is a collaboration of parts that face different directions & move independently & being in love with her was one of the most complicated things I have ever felt.

Sea-Witch is a feeling of loss. When I lived in Sea-Witch I left my hands dirty & my hair dirtier. It hung down in my face & when it didn't I would adjust it to make sure it did. The various positions of my bodies were different words: mountain, sand, sadness, frustration, defeat, shrub. When I lived in Sea-Witch I communicated this way & when I communicated I communicated only with myself & with Sea-Witch, who is a part of me. When I lived in Sea-Witch I sang songs about love & imagined them sung to me.

I am crying because Sea-Witch is crying.

Sea-Witch, you are not swimming. You are held underwater until you stop kicking. When it goes black you see amber clouds shaped like the people you love. The people you wanted to love. I have lost myself like this too, & I, living inside her at the time, understood. But I knew in my understanding that I would never understand. I walked around my living space lying facedown on all the floors. Lying facedown by the bed. Lying facedown in the kitchen. Lying facedown in the bathroom. Understanding is not something you can just have, but you can suffer from both understanding & not. Loving a girl in Sea-Witch, even yourself, requires a kind of bone death.

In Sea-Witch I never knew when I was having sex. Some bodies don't lend themselves to a clear separation of beginning or end & in some bodies that separation is too great. Exhausting, even. Mine has always been some combination of both. Sex happens in Sea-Witch by taking "turns". Each participant gets a turn, followed by the other participant's turn. Turns can look like anything & can take any amount of time. Whole months have been spent on a single turn. A turn can be a pause, the drawing of certain symbols in mud, or nearly endless tears. Most of my turns in Sea-Witch looked the same: creating sound as quietly as possible near my lover's hair or skin. If there is no sound to be made or hair or skin to be found in the particular bodies we are inhabiting I am usually satisfied with anything I can connect to the concept of "closest". This is why my thoughts are shaped in the way they are now. Why draw symbols when you can use all of who you are. When you can act as one yourself.

The following is a list of facts about my time in Sea-Witch:

1. When I was living in Sea-Witch I organized my life around the same principles many people living in Sea-Witch did. The most important of those was When they come for us, we will climb the trees. This one is very old & the origin is unknown. I don't think anyone ever told me about it. When you get to Sea-Witch there are certain things you just know.

2. Every night in Sea-Witch I slept deeply until I couldn't sleep anymore. I had a feeling that things happened while I was asleep in Sea-Witch, that my living space, my bed, my lover all changed in small degrees, an entire revolution until they arrived back where they were before I fell asleep. I also felt as if some nights didn't make it the full way around. They felt too almost.

3. Everyone in Sea-Witch used to drown themselves in waves a lot. It was something to do to pass the time, which is a really difficult thing to measure in Sea-Witch. We found the ocean for this under our beds. The ocean in Sea-Witch is still there, under all the beds & all of Sea-Witch knows they can drown themselves in it at any time, but they don't. They just think about it.

4. At one point while I was living in Sea-Witch we all sat down for a very long time & looked at grass. All of my best memories of Sea-Witch are from this time, but it had to end eventually.

5. The whole time I was living Sea-Witch I kept a stone in my pocket wrapped in old paper I tore from a book & held together with hair ties. Every night I would wash it in Sea-Witch's hair & feed it bits of mushroom & herbs, whatever I had around. When I spoke to it I felt listened to. Before I left Sea-Witch I gave this rock to Sea-Witch as a present, & she ate it, saying I will keep it safe here. I wrote her a thank you note & signed it with all my names. I kissed Sea-Witch & felt the rock moving inside. When they come for us, we will climb the trees.

it is because
of herself
that she is
called
"sea"

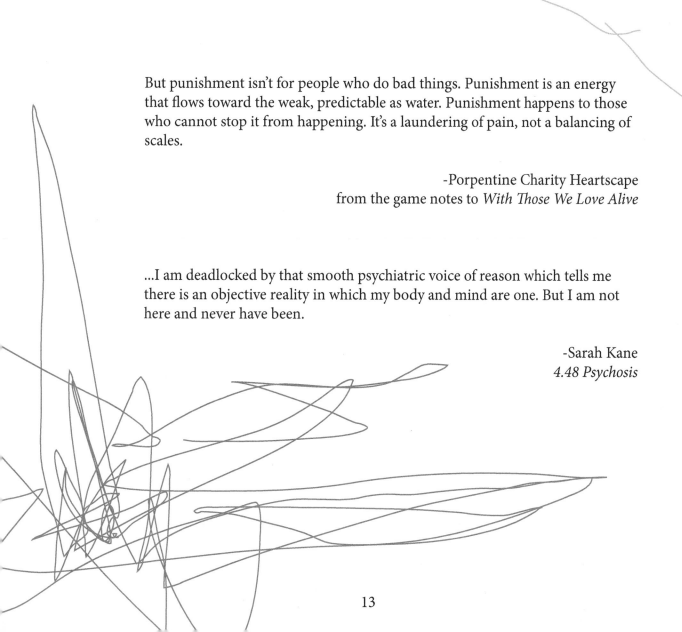

But punishment isn't for people who do bad things. Punishment is an energy that flows toward the weak, predictable as water. Punishment happens to those who cannot stop it from happening. It's a laundering of pain, not a balancing of scales.

-Porpentine Charity Heartscape
from the game notes to *With Those We Love Alive*

...I am deadlocked by that smooth psychiatric voice of reason which tells me there is an objective reality in which my body and mind are one. But I am not here and never have been.

-Sarah Kane
4.48 Psychosis

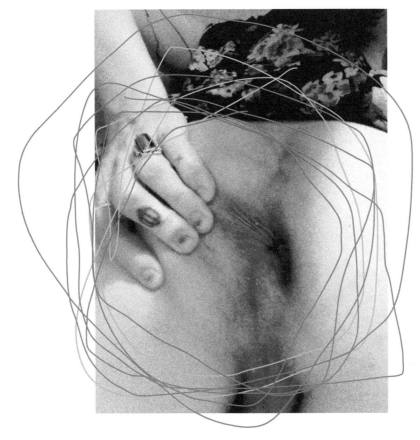

"L'Origin du Monde"

Sea-Witch is a problem of sizes. I fit so well in Sea-Witch, but things that fit in me before can't seem to follow. I am not yet sure what I am a problem of. I brought everything I own to the beach & put it on a raft & conveniently forgot to get on the raft with it. Then the ocean floated away from us both. I sat down right there & tried to figure out the whole thing on paper. I made a variable that represented the whole situation (me, the ocean, the raft), a second variable that represented the distant influence of Meteor (may she lay us waste) & a third that represented the concept of loss or displacement. I spent a long time creating charts & proofs that would help me understand the barrier that had been created between myself & Sea-Witch. I began cutting away the unnecessary parts from the mess I had created, on the assumption that they must have come only from myself. I was left with a statement that I realized described a small aspect of the nature of Sea-Witch. Living in Sea-Witch for so long had left me endlessly tired & I could not remember if I had been tired before I lived in Sea-Witch. In Sea-Witch I could hold my own loneliness in my hand & feel its fur. I could cut it open on a sharp rock. More often I put it under my mattress & clenched my teeth so hard while I slept that my jaw stayed sore.

People have asked me about this so I'll try to answer. Same-sex marriage is not legal in Sea-Witch but also not illegal. This is because you will quickly find out in Sea-Witch that no sex is the same. As I've said before, sex is made up of "turns". Turns can look like anything, but they are never the same. Something always changes. Our cells are always cycling difference.

Also I want to talk about the word "legal" which doesn't make a lot of sense in Sea-Witch. Other words whose meanings don't hold together within Sea-Witch's person include deserve, crime, alphabet, drug, animal, border & joke. One time Sea-Witch told a joke about a very large dog & the very large dog showed up & we realized it wasn't a joke. She was just telling us about the dog. The dog stayed for a long time.

History tells us Sea-Witch is a girl. It says Sea-Witch was not born a boy (which is a strange thing to have to emphasize) but a girl with a girl's teeth & fingers. It tells us of how she ingested plants, fungi & chemicals to alter her body in ways that she felt might make her body & mind become closer to herself. She later came to dismiss some of these things as having undesirable effects & others she held dearly as sacraments. During our hardest times or certain positions of the planets we would eat some of these in the presence of the image of a living goddess. In the image she is nineteen years old, wearing her sister's sports bra, which is stuffed with her own dirty socks. She is peering at herself in the bathroom mirror while no one else is home. Sea-Witcheans carved her holy image fifty-feet high into a mountain & called her meteor. Sea-Witch calls her home.

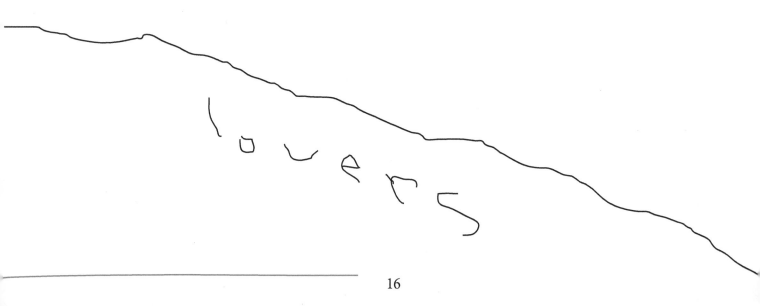

SEA-WITCH 10

After I left Sea-Witch I mourned. I mourned her loss as well as my own. There are no words to say the things I want to say. There is no way to express the feeling of separation when you are choosing that separation against love. I admit now that I loved Sea-Witch. I admit that her sadness gave me comfort in my sadness. Loving one who worships her own destruction is a hopeless act. It isn't the only hopeless thing I have ever done, & in a way it is not one I regret. She will always be my most beautiful. & so I mourn.

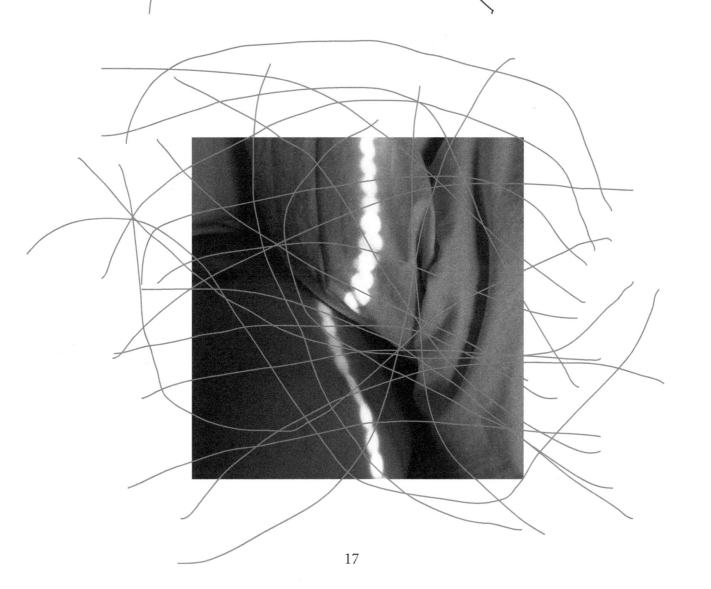

I am all of Sea-Witch & I hold her inside me. Even now, years later, I find myself doing things in the Sea-Witch custom. I find myself carrying her inside of me. If you don't know what I mean, let me try to explain:

1. Sea-Witch is full of death. She eats dead plants & dirt & has thrown herself more than one party. Sea-Witch brushes her hair from her forehead as she takes a dog* for a walk & smokes while it shits at 3:47 a.m..

2. Sea-Witch is the name of the water from my melting. She is the thing I hold when the ground feels too wide not to fall into.

3. Some monsters have found themselves spontaneously in the presence of Sea-Witch under the influence of alcohol & singing. Such encounters are not unheard of.

4. Sea-Witch is a nucleus of pain. Sea-Witch is not the source of the pain, but she receives it from what can seem like everywhere. The source of Sea-Witch's pain is seventy-eight men who are the source of a great deal of pain in the world. One can get very rich by creating pain in others. In fact, it is the only way to become rich. Some of these men are very famous, they appear on television with their thin hair & stubby fingers. Others seem to be invisible, anonymous, but intimidatingly so. It is because of these men & the pain they make that Sea-Witch first invited us into her body, many years ago. It is because of these men & the pain they make that the mass of pure inevitability we call Meteor (may she lay us waste) approaches. It is because of them that Sea-Witch is called "Witch". It is because of herself that she is called "Sea".

5. I made a boat out of wood & sailed it into the ocean. Once I was far enough out that I could no longer see land I made a symbol on my hand with mud I had carried there in a jar. When nothing seems real it can help to remember there is no agreed-upon idea about what is real & what is not. What we know as reality exists only through collaboration & sharing & you are in no way required to live there.

---

* A note on the word "dog", which I have found is unspecific in its use. When I was living in Sea-Witch some of us were smaller & covered in fur, & preferred to spend cold nights lying across the sleeping legs of the taller, hairless Sea-Witcheans. All of us made sounds at the fullest moons &, though she was not visible at the time, to distant Meteor (may she lay us waste). All of us enjoy sleeping in laps.

The experience of living outside of Sea-Witch has been, for me, a sensation like being slowly crumpled from the outside in. Breathing becomes difficult & muscles contain a constant, slowing fatigue. I have said that I was born in Sea-Witch, that I am always inside her & have always been. This is true but in the same way I have always been outside her & always have felt a distance, a longing & its accompanying external pressure. _____

Before I lived in Sea-Witch I had a dream about a field of small animals who hid their faces from the sun. I walked among them & touched the leaves that hung down from nearby trees. There was in this dream, as in others, a looming sense of something like disaster.

I, like Sea-Witch, am a monster. I will one day be slain by the crushing, which comes from everywhere, but originates from the choices of the seventy-eight men I have mentioned elsewhere. When I was young I imagined that I could live among people in the world. I was afraid of monsters because I did not know that they were my kind. I was also afraid of monsters because I knew they were my kind, & looking at yourself & seeing what you are afraid of will always be terrifying.

When I left home I got drunk in the sand for four days. A star looked at me & said everything will be okay. I said that, no, it wouldn't. It said that I was right, but that it wished I was wrong. I said I wished it too. There wasn't anything to say after that, & I kept it's gaze too long, sitting in an embarrassed silence.

The next day I laid my fear at the feet of Sea-Witch, to whom I had fled, & lit that fear on fire. I slept beside that fire for two nights, until she invited me inside her body. This was the beginning of the next part of my life. I've found I can best organize my life in my own mind by the kind of fear I was experiencing at the time, & this was the start of a new, special fear.

I cut my body into little suns

Sea-Witch held me after my formation. I cried in her arms & in her hair & went into her body through the entrance to her body, which is the ear. When I got there I met others for whom she had done the same. I saw their beautiful faces & hair & how they covered them with dirt like I had covered mine with dirt. They took me to a beach there where I could live. Sea-Witch is one of the few places in the world where the act of living & doing the few things that are needed to live hasn't been made so difficult as to be nearly impossible. Outside of Sea-Witch you have to be nearly obsessed with doing a lot of very specific strange things at the service of the seventy-eight men who cause pain & you have to spend much of your life doing & thinking about these things in order to live, & even then, even if you focus your whole self on this service you still often will not be able to live. For those of us who are monsters this will always be so difficult as to be nearly impossible. I can't tell you how it is for those who are not monsters, because I do not know how to speak to them. In Sea-Witch living is everywhere. It doesn't eat you from within.

I'm not sure people exist. I often think about myself & the time I spent in the world among people before I came to Sea-Witch. About the time before I knew I was a monster. People is the word for living creatures who look almost like monsters but not quite. People can be found almost everywhere, but I always wonder if they aren't maybe, secretly, monsters too.

When I arrived at Sea-Witch for the first time, I told her I am so tired now. I said, I am tired & tired of being tired. She told me to come in & sleep. I told her I could sleep for lifetimes & then I did just that.

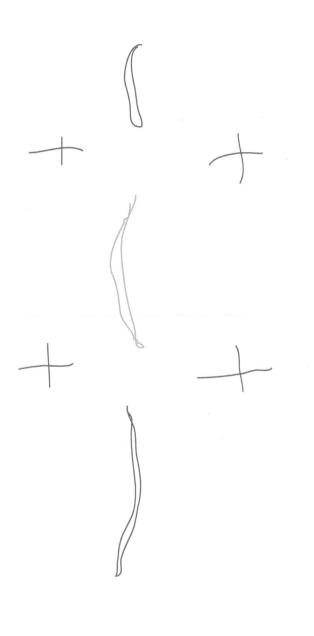

22

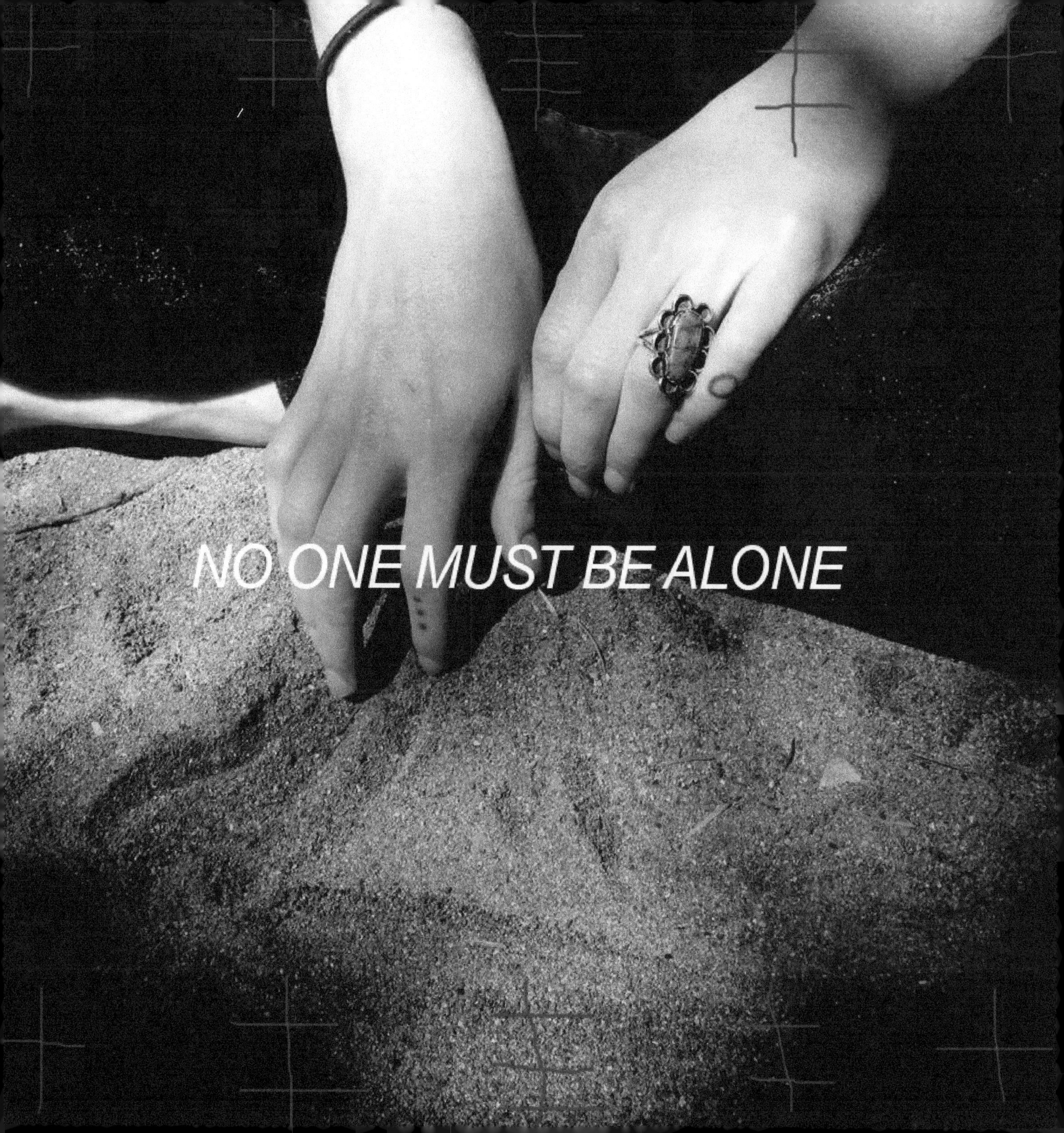
NO ONE MUST BE ALONE

there's an illiteracy between our legs
where parts of me are you
and parts of you are me

- Jordaan Mason & the Horse Museum
"The Wrong Parts (Vivian Sisters Singing)"

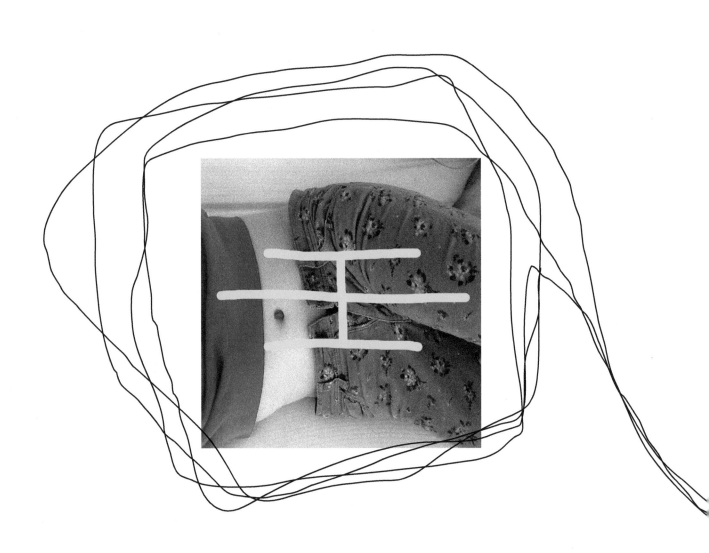

Sea-Witch is one of a series. People speak of other Sea-Witches & there are ways in which different parts of Sea-Witch are their own separate beings & are referred to as such, but apart from this there is some knowledge of her companions in series, which is held in the Book of Meteor. The Book of Meteor tells us before Sea-Witch was formed there existed Dog-Witch & hir sisters. At this point there was no land & so no word for "sea", which only exists in contrast with land. "Water" existed & meant "everything-except-air". Things under the water were referred to as "airless faces". Dog-Witch & hir sisters are named variously throughout The Book of Meteor as Air-Witch, Water-Witch, Dirt-Witch, & Milk-Witch, Deeps-Witch, Old Seagull-Witch, Strawberry-Witch, Leg-Witch, Candle-Witch, Less-Held-Witch, Moss-Witch, Dead-Jellyfish-Witch, Stone-Witch, Wood-Witch, Glass-Witch, Airless-Face-Witch & her twin God-Witch, Death-Witch & some texts speak of a nineteenth sister whose name is written "ha-ha-ha" or "ah-ah-ah", pronounced as three brief puffs of air, with or without accompanying glottal stops.

Dog-Witch, of course, initiated the formation of hir sisters & their deaths. Ze gave us meteor (may she lay us waste) & her book. What Sea-Witcheans have learned about Dog-Witch is that ze caused the formation of the nineteen after ze stole lava from an airless face that most Sea-Witcheans refer to as a bear. A thing I have discovered while reading the Book of Meteor & other Sea-Witchean lore is that there have always been bears. Even before land there were bears in the water, though they had longer faces & thick, flat hands & feet like beaver tails. Lava, before it was taken by Dog-Witch, was a piece of ancient bear technology that the bears used to control other airless faces & the water around them. The bears have mourned its loss ever since the theft. Sea-Witcheans who study this history do so to try to find a time before this sort of controlling of other beings existed, so that we might know its source & overthrow the seventy-eight men. It has not yet been discovered, though we have determined this source is deeper than lava.

Dog-Witch has always seemed untouchable in my mind. On one of the long nights in the hardest months, Sea-Witch & I were up late sharing a cigarette & she told me how much she misses hir. I asked what Dog-Witch looked like & she smiled sadly & described to me a sensation I would later come to call bone death. She told me about Dog-Witch's long, furry ears & hir face like a dry, cavernous world of old stone & gas. She made a series of gestures in the air & drew this symbol in the sand. After this she took my head in her lap & stroked my hair & said to me "No one must be alone."

Like everything, all of Sea-Witch contains her history. Every part of her has bits of what has come before. For example, Sea-Witch's left leg is the same as that of Dog-Witch. That leg was out of reach to Sea-Witcheans for a great number of years. Sea-Witch has allowed us her body for living in, but there was a time in which she wasn't sure about the her-ness of that leg, & for that reason alone kept it free of residents. Not for reasons of property, which is a concept that, like many other concepts, can't hold together within Sea-Witch, but for reasons of body & consent. Dog-Witch, being maybe-dead after the fall of the nineteen, could not consent to her leg being occupied, even while it was a part of Sea-Witch's person. On the day that Sea-Witch finally set fire to a dead fir tree as a ritual of mourning, she accepted that leg as her own & Sea-Witcheans came to the leg & created in it there as a sanctuary for the oldest & most desperate among us to live & rest on the beaches that could be found there. The skies there are full of stars that are visible at all hours & form constellations of welcome & refuge.

The Book of Meteor tells us Dog-Witch is a sense of purpose. It tells us of how ze came from the sky as fire & evaporated a great deal of water, creating land. It tells us of hir cooling & descent again into the water to struggle against the violent reign of the lava-wielding bears in the world of airless faces. It tells us how ze brought lava to new uses, the foremost of which is formation, including the formation of hir nineteen sisters, who were the first to be formed in lava, as I would later be. The first of hir sisters to be formed was called Deeps-Witch & shortly after came Dirt-Witch & Bread-Witch. Less-Held-Witch stood from the sand next, & pulled with her the twins God-Witch & Airless-Face-Witch. A passage missing from some later translations of the Book tells us Dog-Witch came to these sisters then on the land, hir tail & ears raised, excited to no longer be alone. Ze lay hir chin on them one by one, naming each as hir love, hir sibling, hir comrade & hir companion. The other sisters formed soon after, the order is not fully documented. It is written that angry bears soon came & lined the coast, watching Dog-Witch & hir glorious creation take shape from the ruins of their fallen empire. Bear-parents stroked the shoulders & heads of their furry children saying to them, The time will come when we can build ourselves up again.

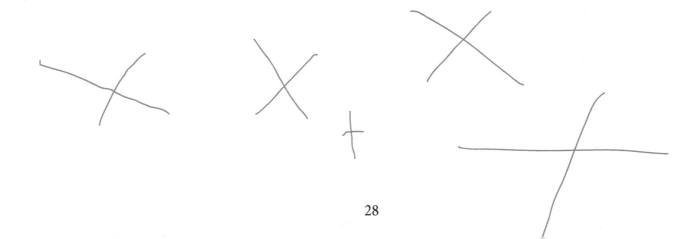

BONE DEATH 5

A beautiful space opened up in the earth in which many events took place. A necessary part of formation, besides lava, is noticing. Less-Held-Witch began her noticing here in this space, where she was attending a class on the ghosts who animate fire. It was in this beautiful space where she first noticed the curve of Glass-Witch's neck as she sat against the wall, ignoring the lecture to draw round sigils on the white spaces of her purple tennis shoes. It was in this space that the Book of Meteor tells us Less-Held-Witch hid herself in the hood of her sweatshirt, looking down at her own shoes (brown, soft) to avoid Glass-Witch's gaze.

I know from my own formation that noticing has a heaviness to it that follows you. It sits in your chest & shoulders. The object of your noticing becomes transformed entirely in your mind, becomes a thing to worship. You become transformed as well. The wholeness of who you were forms into a halfness of what you could become.

Sometime after her first noticing, the book of Meteor tells us, Glass-Witch & Less-Held-Witch began to spend lunches together, eating. They spoke quietly, of the others in their class. Less-Held-Witch did most of the listening, wholly absorbed in her own noticing. Glass-Witch said to her once, in the context of a conversation, You are the kind of girl who most don't think to fall for. But those who do, fall deeply.

Long after Less-Held-Witch finished that class she wore purple shoes upon which she drew round sigils in ball-point pen. She wrote songs to sing to other living creatures. Some of these songs spoke of histories that had never been written down. Others were written to sing to a nameless thing she felt always growing in the dirt that she never found, despite her great noticing.

From what is known of the history, most Sea-Witcheans believe that the nineteen sisters spread from the coast where their forming was initiated, across all land & water. They lived full lives as whole individuals. There was once a television show about these stories, but it has been lost to time. What has been written of this show tells us that this was no great loss.

FULK

Cypionate

SHE GETS COLD LIKE ALL LIVING CREATURES

actual photo

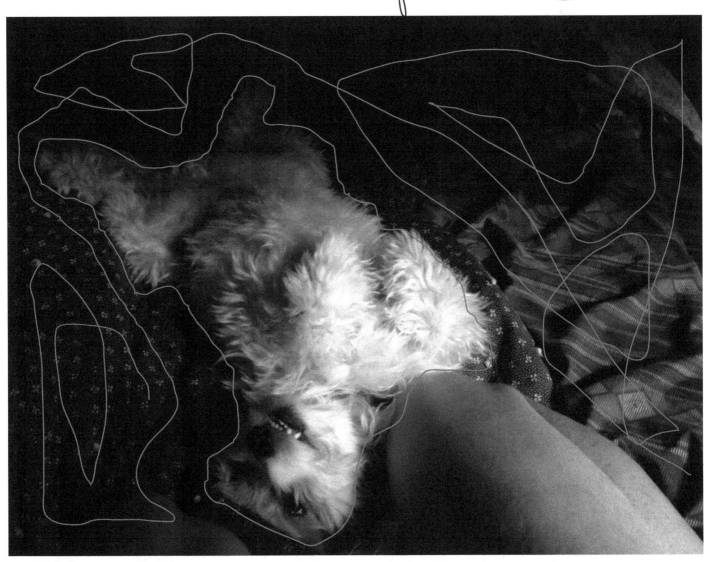

of Dog-Witch

Purity; not all encompassing, perhaps not immediately recognized, but the core presides within, and is the compass of all action to its bearer. There are those who exist who believe in and try to achieve purity as a fluid becoming, while not ever having pureness at their core.

-Danielle Lee Pearce
from the album notes to *Petrichor*

TRANS MEMOIR 8

Everything was lava for a while, really. This was before Sea-Witch, & everything was on fire & lava & I was on fire & lava myself, being one small part, one aspect of that everything. A lot of sensations have been compared to burning, like the feeling you get in your lungs when holding your breath too long. A lot of what happened then took place in my lungs, which are two parallel sites of construction & destruction of atmosphere. Lava began to feel very atmospheric.

There is a story, many stories actually, told among those in Sea-Witch about a girl who tried to cool with her mouth the lava around another girl. One of those stories ends with the destruction of lava as a concept. Another ends with her lying in a field of grass, holding a living creature she has vowed to care for in whatever ways she can. This sense of care goes on to flow outward from her & envelops every living thing, & every living thing cares for & respects every other living thing. Care is a desired ending, but one that cannot be obtained without an intense, even violent period of restructuring.

Sea-Witch can go for long periods of time without eating. She emits a specific light & temperature. Sea-Witch is a glittering cascade of water that has frozen in place exactly to be lived in but accidentally ended up capable of true emotion. Sea-Witch is precious & needs to be held. She gets cold like all living creatures.

The Book of Meteor contains only some information about the life of Air-Witch. It tells of how a young Air-Witch first found a place for herself within a community of rats. How she slept in their tangle every night, & they shared with her their garbage, which she learned to eat & love. The rats taught her how to gnaw her way into crawlspaces & behind pantries. They taught her how to keep from being seen. Air-Witch's body did not look like the bodies of the rats, but this was no problem. Air-Witch didn't think about her body. This isn't about Air-Witch's body. This isn't about anybody's body. This is about the bodies of rats & how Air-Witch cried when she came home one day to find those bodies twitching, nearly lifeless on the ground. This is about how Air-Witch killed one of her family trying to save them with her large, clumsy hands. How Air-Witch then cut herself & bled on the floor & cried & how her tears became tiny ambulances that flowed their way through the blood to save her family, each arriving just seconds too late.

Air-Witch went from that place to a mountain where she lived alone, because living alone, while it made her very strange, felt like the only thing she knew how to do. She could barely feed herself during this time. She ate dirt & insects & bark & leaves. She vomited on herself when she slept at night & became too weak most days to move far. The first time she died she left herself a note that said "don't eat the leaves with the zigzag edges." The second time she died she left a note with various ideas about how she might teach herself to grow wings, which she managed to do before the third time she died. It took until after the fifth time she died to figure out how to fly with the wings. Once she was confident in her flying Air-Witch took a large piece of birch bark & wrote out with berry ink a letter to Dog-Witch. Air-Witch had been alone for a long time at this point & her mind worked in strange ways. The letter failed completely at communicating anything, but Air-Witch buried it there, just in case. After this was done, Air-Witch flew into the sky as high as she could. Some say she went to find meteor (may she lay us waste). Some say after she spent so long alone she no longer understood what she or her body was doing. That she probably fell into the sea & drowned. Her letter was never found, & most likely crumbled into the dirt as it was buried. The Sea-Witchean Church of Meteor claims it has Air-Witch's wings among its holy objects, embalmed & stiff & kept in a locked case in a locked room no one ever enters.

BONE DEATH 11-26

It is written that Dog-Witch died on the day Air-Witch left for the sky.

39

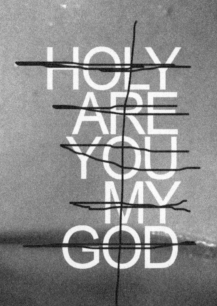

HOLY
ARE
YOU
MY
GOD

DAUGHTER

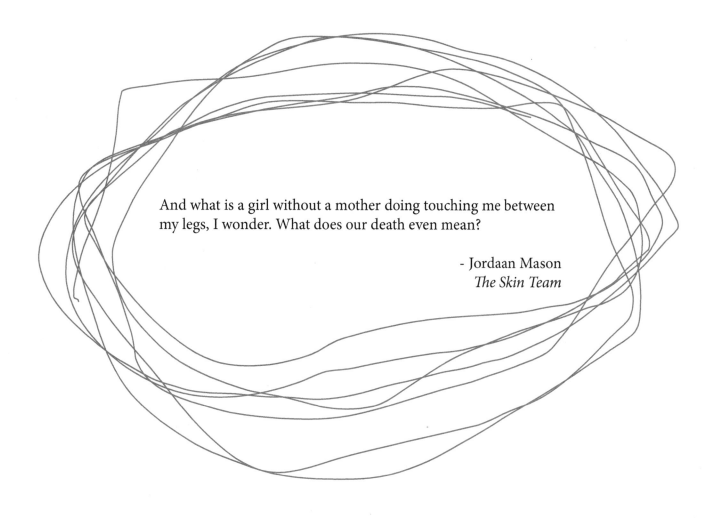

And what is a girl without a mother doing touching me between my legs, I wonder. What does our death even mean?

- Jordaan Mason
The Skin Team

> milk-witch was round
> & did a lot of warm dialing
> all those little number buttons
> in the mouths of infants
>
> *-author unknown*

The Book of Meteor contains a short list of facts about Dog-Witch's sister Milk-Witch, & I have duplicated this list below, with a few of my own additions & notes:

1. Milk-Witch had many infants she kept warm in blankets. She bathed them regularly in the hot springs. She kept a rigorous kind of schedule. When she was young she would sometimes shut herself in the closet with the infants until they would whimper so that she could take delight in comforting them.

2. Milk-Witch hated getting mad. She was always shocking herself by raising her voice. "I will not be loud & mean," she would say, over & over again until she fell asleep.

3. Sometimes in the morning Milk-Witch forgot to shave her face. She wouldn't realize until later, when everything was hard. On these days she would try to think of herself as a single protein, drifting through blood without thought or feeling. All Milk-Witch's being was sustained by the effort of a small group of ghosts, & these days took the whole of their attention & effort.

4. Milk-Witch had t-shirts made of her & the infants. Everybody got one. The Sea-Witchean Church of Meteor has one of these shirts in their collection of holy artifacts. They also have one of the infants. She runs the gift shop & splits the income with the ones who make the gifts. In Sea-Witch, gifts are made or found by all living creatures. A gift can be almost anything. For example, this book is my gift to you.

5. Milk-Witch had a collection of broken glass in a box in her room. The glass pieces had names & Milk-Witch would sometimes break them so she could name more pieces & have more friends. When she lost a piece, she would try to make herself forget its name. It never worked.

6. Mid-way through her life, Milk-Witch had the most beautiful surgery in the whole world.

7. Milk-Witch was one of the rare living creatures whose life ended when she decided it was time for her life to end. She spent years making this decision & when the time got closer, she told her infants & they talked about it for a long time. They all sat on the beach together, throwing rocks into the waves. They

meant to stay up all night but the infants didn't quite make it, & slept their infant sleeps in the cool night sand. In the morning, Milk-Witch nudged them awake. "It's time to go now," she told them, & they woke up & began to cry. "It's time to go," she said again.

BONE DEATH 29

The Book of Meteor says that true to her name, Death-Witch died young, against her will. She was known by few, & mourned long by those who knew her. She was survived by her best friend, a nameless cat who went on to lead a full life for many years after.

The circumstances surrounding Death-Witch's death are that she was alone on a road, & a person saw what she looked like & decided to kill her. I guess that's all it takes. There is a lot of anger in the world, & sometimes I think I feel all of it at once when I think about what happened to little Death-Witch.

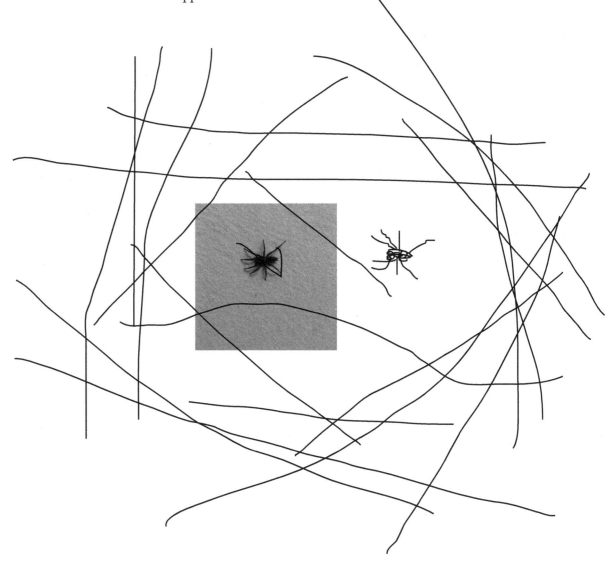

BONE DEATH SUN

Dirt-Witch was beautiful & she loved horses. She spent her entire childhood putting her fingers in the gaps on an oak leaf & her teen years were mostly spitting into a jar of sand. She had twelve family members who were given to her on a boat as a present from a thirteenth family member she never met. She kept them in a backpack. One time one of the family members got caught by the dog & its ear started to split at the seam & some stuffing came out but Dirt-Witch was her own mom & fixed the family member with a needle & thread. When Dirt-Witch got older she coughed into the sky & thought about girls. She went to a school for a very long time & got out later. She tried to make movies about the way she loved horses when she was younger but they never turned out right, because her skin was too soft to hold the camera. Because the ground was too soft to hold her up. Dirt-Witch is my mother & I am her daughter, even though we have never met. We have ten alikenesses that Sea-Witch told me about later. The first four are all horse sounds. When I think of Dirt-Witch it makes me want to pray forever.

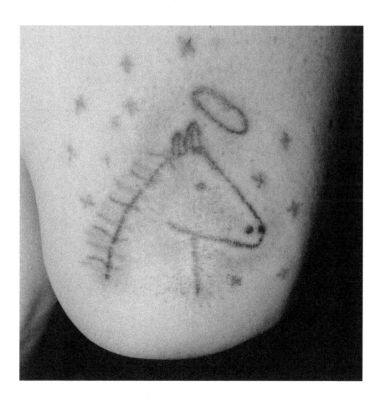

All of my strength is found in Sea-Witch. Her name means longing. I hold her in my arms the way she held me forever since I have first come to live inside her. On the fourth day after my arrival in her person I woke up to find a pit at the foot of my bed, filled fifteen feet deep with rotting dresses. It was early enough that Sea-Witch was still asleep & so I looked into it & prayed to meteor (may she lay us waste) as is customary upon waking in Sea-Witch. Meteor (may she lay us waste) prayed back to me & asked me what this pit was here for. She prayed to me asking what I planned to use it for. I don't know, I prayed back. It smells.

Questions:

    1. If I dive headfirst into a pit that is filled 15 feet deep with dresses, what will happen to my neck?

    2. If I don't dive in, what will happen to my neck?

    3. Is it possible to have sex with a meteor god (may she lay us waste)?

    4. Is it possible to do so via prayer?

Just in case I took my underwear off, which I had slept in.

    What are you doing right now, I prayed to meteor (may she lay us waste).

    Oh, not much, she prayed back. I got this CD, she prayed to me.

    Oh yeah? I prayed back. What is it?

    Some band, she prayed to me. They're called Girls With Assholes.

    Cool, I prayed. I love Girls With Assholes.

    Yeah, she prayed. Me too.

    I giggled. I wish you were here right now, I prayed.

    You would be dead if I were there, Meteor (msluw) prayed back.

    I know, but we could have sex, I prayed.

    We can have sex now. I felt her prayer on my skin.

Questions:

1. What if I am bad at this?
2. How do I know if it's my turn?
3. Should I have sex inside the pit of rotting dresses?
4. What is Sea-Witch doing right now?
5. What are the names of the members in the band Girls With Assholes?
6. What if we're both bottoms?

She prayed to ask if it was okay if she came inside me. Her flat affect was adorable.
I washed my hands in the dresses & prayed back to her. You are always inside me, I prayed.
Holy are you, my god, I prayed.
Holy are you, my god, she prayed back.

We took our turns from there, pushing skin aside & braiding hair. I made my sounds on her, all of my closest &
she gave me her prayers from her place among the stars. I set the dresses on fire & sweated in their heat. I kept my
sweat for meteor (msluw) & we had there a communion of fluids. She cried out loud & the stars watched & winked
at our soft assholes. We prayed back & forth apart from time. We spent ourselves enough (but never enough!) & sat
in our silence. I found my thoughts drifting to Sea-Witch, who never woke, but slept soundly all through. Holy are
you, my god, I thought.

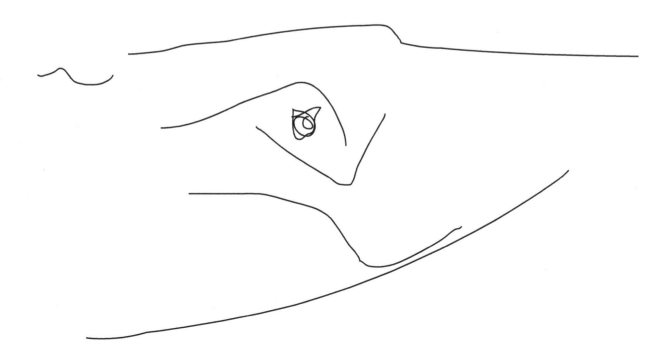

50

hold well
nothing is pure

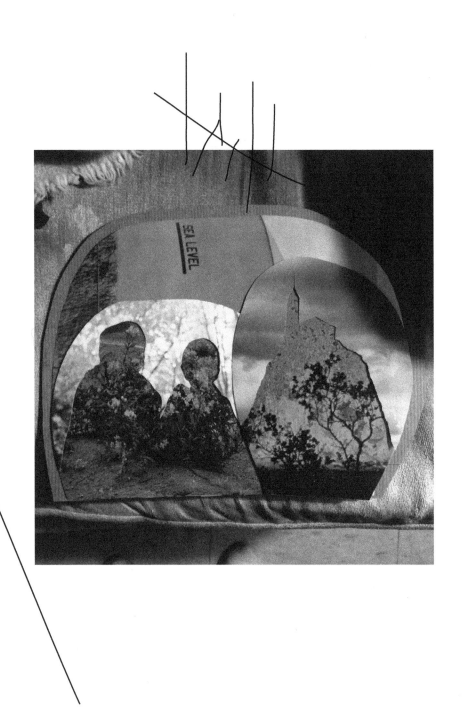

[T]he strange thing, the thing that you can never explain to anyone, except another nut, or, if you're lucky, a doctor who has an unusual amount of sense—stranger than the hallucinations, or the voices, or the anxiety—is the way you begin to experience the edges of the mind itself...in a way other people just can't.

- Samuel R. Delany
Dhalgren

dddddddddddddddddddddddddddddddddddddddddddddddddddddddddddddddddddddddddddddddddddddddddddd
dddddddddddddddddddddddddddddddddddddddddddddddddddddddddddddddddddddddddddddddddddddddddddd
dddddddddddddddddddddddddddddddddddddddddddddddddddddddddddddddddddddddddddddddddddddddddddd
dddddddddddddddddddddddddddddddddddddddddddddddddddddddddddddddddddddddddddddddddddddddddddd
ddddddddddddddddddddddddddddddddddddddddddddddddddddddddddddddddddddddddddddddddddddddddddd

ddddddddddddddddddddddddddddddddddddddddddddddddddddddddddddddddd

dddddddddddddddddddddddddddddddddddddddddddddddddd

dddddddddddddddddddddddddddddddddddddddddddddddddddddddddddddddddddddddddd

dddddddddddddddddddddddddddddddddddddddddddddddddddddddddddddddddddddddddddddddddddddddddddd
dddddddddddddddddddddddddddddddddddddddddddddddddddddddddddddddddddddddddddddddddddddddddddd
dddddddddddddddddddddddddddddddddddddddddddddddddddddddddddddddddddddddddddddddddddddddddddd
dddddddddddddddddddddddddddddddddddddddddddddddddddddddddddddddddddddddddddddddddddddddddddd
dddddddddddddddddddddddddddddddd

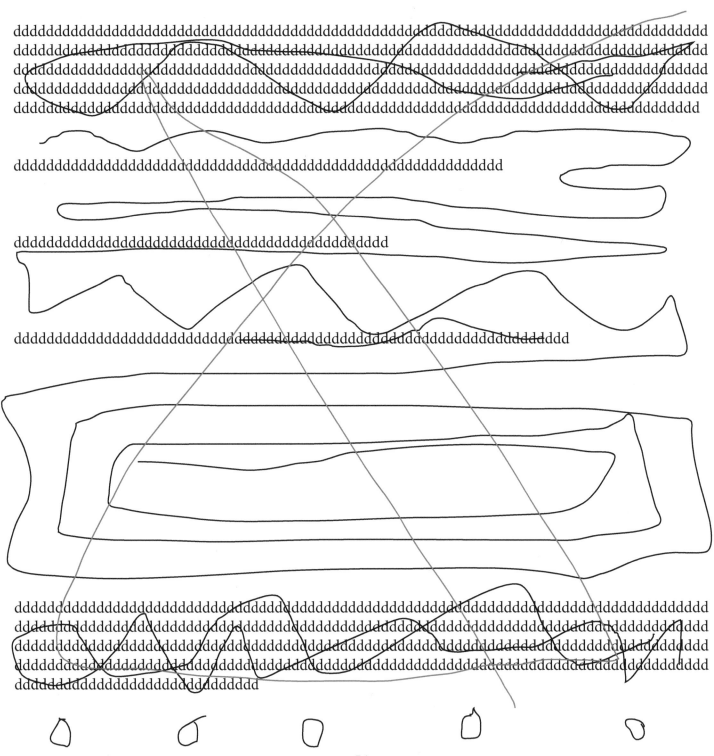

BONE DEATH []

Old-Seagull-Witch spent her time in the laboratory at the University of Crater, where she transcribed messages from the feet of insects. The insects used their feet to ask questions about pain that didn't have clear answers. On her lunch breaks, Old-Seagull-Witch ate soft sandwiches from the vending machine. She talked to her girlfriend, who stayed at home to write down stories about pain, on the telephone. Sometimes they texted. There were six living creatures who lived in the woods outside of the laboratory. One tuesday they slipped a piece of paper under the door of the laboratory that said

> Dear Pain Researchers,
>
> We held one of ourselves & watched her die. She grew fleshy tufts on her body after five
> days. We ate the tufts & her body lost itself in the woods. You have to find her body.
> We think it got lost in your pain. Please return it to us. It is okay if you eat any tufts you
> find. Those are for sharing.

It was unsigned. Old-Seagull-Witch was texting about this to her girlfriend when the power went out in the laboratory & all around town. The outage was made for fun by a minor god of pain, who was part insect. The god's outages, if plotted on a map, might say some words. They might read "boys aren't real." Old-Seagull-Witch texted to her girlfriend that she was thinking about her clit. About both of their clits, held together in a gentle fist.

On my nineteenth day in Sea-Witch I had made plans to meet her near the drainage ditch on the other side of the beach parkinglot. I found old, disused cars in there & as I walked past, some of them married us there in the parkinglot sand. I guess I should specify that by "us" I am referring to myself, to all my selves. What I mean is that by the time I arrived at the drainage ditch to meet Sea-Witch there were four of myself, walking on sixteen limbs & going by a collection of names. What I mean to say is that when we got there Sea-Witch held our faces & took our hands & baptized them in the drainage ditch.

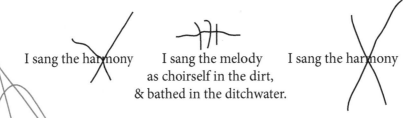

I sang the harmony   I sang the melody   I sang the harmony
                       as choirself in the dirt,
                       & bathed in the ditchwater.

A CROW EMERGED FROM MY HANDS WHEN SEA-WITCH PULLED THEM OUT.

I was all outline   We were all outline
& ghost, pushing   & ghost, pushing
my boundaries   our boundaries
to blur.   to break.

Sea-Witch returned our hands to deadname, who passed them to us, drying them on xyr skirt.
I thanked xem.
deadname leaned toward us, eclipsing our view of Sea-Witch.
"Hold well," xe said. "Nothing is pure."
Xe stroked xyr hand across my forehead / across my lap & I heard
xyr voice & the sound of the holy parkinglottraffic rising in my
ears until it blended into a high pitched
whine.

I woke up again in Sea-Witch after arriving there covered in lava. The patch of sand I slept on had turned to glass beneath me. Formation as a process is one that never ends. It wakes you up at 5am every morning so that it can continue. I pray to myself for it to end. I pray for myself to end.

I have nothing to fear from monsters. It was people who broke my teeth with rocks. It was men who made them think it was necessary. It was angels who watched me crying & stared when I yelled at them. It was monsters who took me inside their bodies for warmth, pleasure & sustenance. It was me who took the form of thirteen birds & died on the sand in a circle. It was meteor (may she lay us waste) who landed in the circle killing everyone. It was everyone who died. It was everyone who, briefly, was resurrected. It was everyone who immediately died again. It was empty I held in my arms after. It was the future I hold in my arms now & call holy. It was the future I kept inside my drawer with the shirts & pants. It was the microscope I used to figure out what my blood was made of. It was hospitals my blood was made of. It was ambulances I found in my breathing. It was the water that came out when I died. It was the water inside me I left to my children. It was daughters they were called by everyone but their mothers. It was daughter they wrote on their chests in red ink. It was communion they had with my water then. It was me whose face hit the pavement. It was people who broke my teeth with rocks.

how many

On my 30th day in Sea-Witch I found need had grown inside my person to the extent it was filling up most of who I was. I had heard stories of this happening to people. I left Sea-Witch with the hope of need inside me & a flock of living creatures taking turns riding in my arms.

I realized at this time that I thought of myself primarily in relation to other monsters in Sea-Witch. This is still true. In a way, I am only a small part of their whole. I keep them & the thought of withness in a pouch along with sand that I can plant wherever I end up. I can scrape the side of a tree & make tea from the bark & in doing this know the process that created me. The color grass takes in direct sun. The whole sound of limbs stretching. I slept for a time in a hole in the earth that contained nothing. The bareness of it was tangible, & I found myself infatuated with how cold it could make me. It got to the point where moving, even slowly, nearly broke my arms & ribs. When can I leave this place? How does it eat me?

Sea-Witch's heart is made of copper. I've seen it. I used to sleep there. It isn't shaped like anything. I mean, when I look at it my mind can't find shape. Twelve living creatures surround it day & night. They keep it warm in their fur they keep it warm with fires they build from their fur's trimmings. They sing songs at night & the words are the plots of films about old houses. About bedrooms.

1. Seeing the heart of Sea-Witch prepared me for life as a monster.
2. Nothing could have prepared me for life as a monster.
3. There is no life to be had as a monster.
4. The only life to be had is life as a monster.
5. I hold the edges.
6. I sewed the words false purity on my couch.
7. I sewed the word daughter on my couch in red thread.
8. I sewed the word dying on my couch.

The room where Sea-Witch's heart is held is nearly impossible to be in / it is so crowded with fire & living creatures. I used to sleep there but stopped because my skin was covered in burns. I found instead a living area in Sea-Witch's feet where I could put my fabric on the walls & furniture. The living creatures there asked me to stay as their monster & I, for a time, did so.

Stone-Witch found she could fit all of Dog-Witch in her mouth at once. This was only one of the many revelations that came through the unstructured process of play they put each other through between sleeping & waking. During quiet moments, Dog-Witch would gently make & unmake the universe around them as ze stroked the freckles that ran across the back of Stone-Witch's shoulders & neck. The sun exploded again & again, filling the sky with light & unlight in turn.

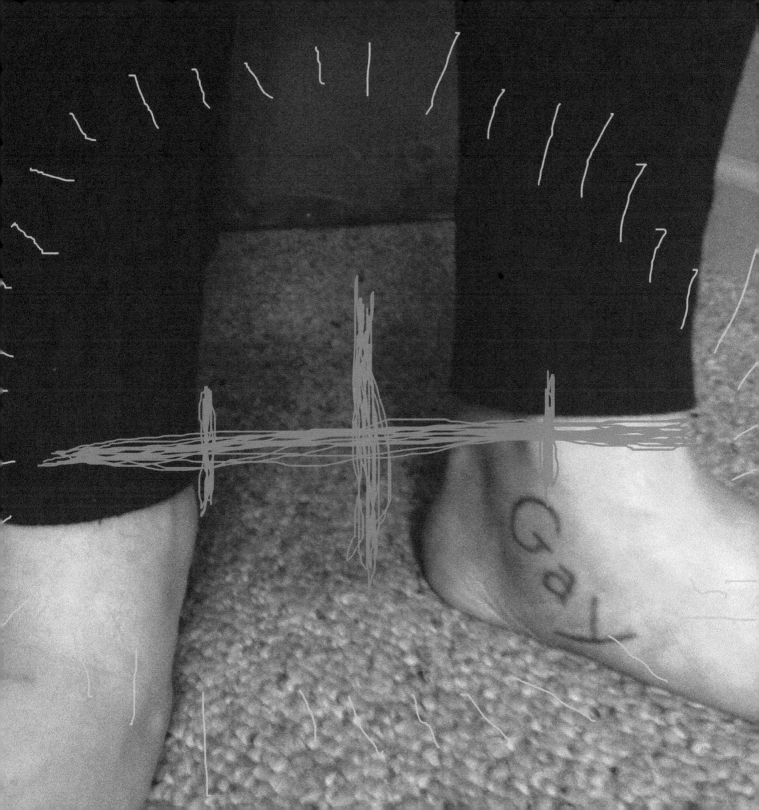

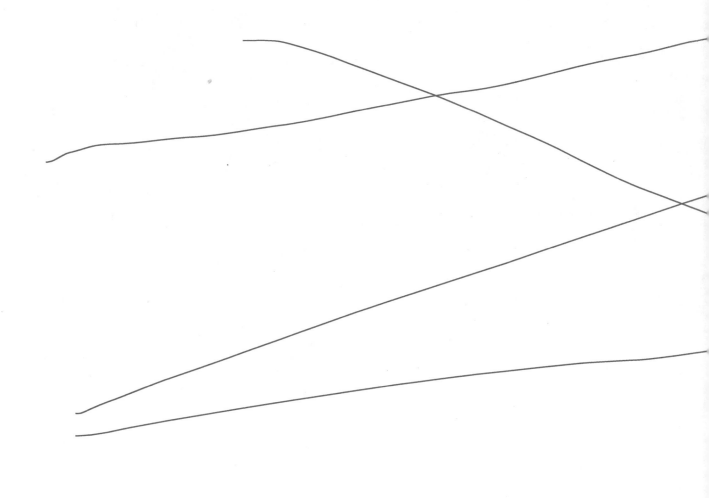

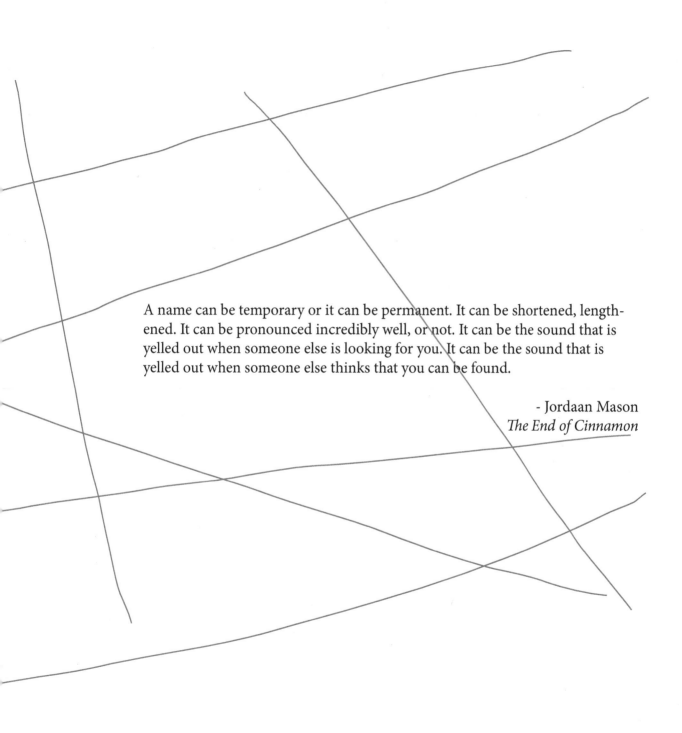

A name can be temporary or it can be permanent. It can be shortened, lengthened. It can be pronounced incredibly well, or not. It can be the sound that is yelled out when someone else is looking for you. It can be the sound that is yelled out when someone else thinks that you can be found.

- Jordaan Mason
The End of Cinnamon

BONE DEATH ??

The Book of Meteor says that Strawberry-Witch first met deadname at a grocery store. She was looking at the beer selection, trying to figure out what to get for the night. deadname asked her where she got her tights. Strawberry-Witch said she couldn't remember. She said maybe they were from a free box, or maybe someone left them over at her house. She said they might have been her ex's. deadname said, Oh. Well thanks anyway. Sure, no problem, Strawberry-Witch said back.

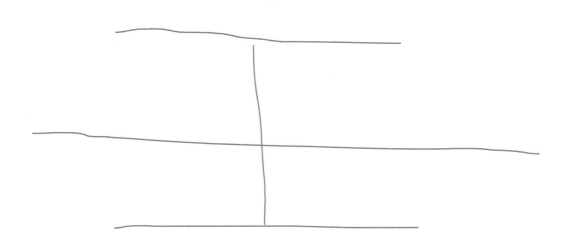

A year later they met again, this time at the bluffs, where Strawberry-Witch had come with two friends. (Some Sea-Witchean scholars suggest these two friends may have been Airless-Face-Witch & ha-ha-ha.) They came to sit & get drunk with the sunset. deadname was there, alone as always, idly digging a small hole in the ground with a stick. Strawberry-Witch noticed xym, but didn't say anything, & deadname didn't approach her either. Strawberry-Witch & her friends quickly got wrapped up in their conversation & their drinking & their sunset & by the time she thought to look again, deadname had gone.

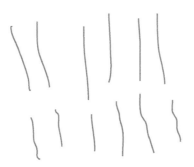

The third time Strawberry-Witch encountered deadname, it was in a dream. The two of them were alone in the stomach of a large, living bird & muscle rippled all around them. As soon as she noticed xym, deadname apologized for coming to see her this way. Xe said could you please follow me & Strawberry-Witch said yes, of course, no mind. Strawberry-Witch, upon waking, couldn't remember where it was that deadname had led her after that.

The fourth & fifth times they met, deadname assumed a familiarity with Strawberry-Witch that xe had never before used. I have been very lonely, xe said on one of these occasions.

deadname began showing up in Strawberry-Witch's life in many small ways after that. She would notice what seemed to be a glimpse of xyr hair in the reflection of a car window. She found an earring she thought xe had been wearing under the couch on her porch. Strawberry-Witch began to leave messages to deadname in the form of small knife scratches on mirrors & floors. Messages that looked like lines & symbols, shapes & holes. deadname communicated back through particularly informational smells that seemed to have no source, & ideas that would occur with a certain parallel nature she associated with deadname's face & expressions.

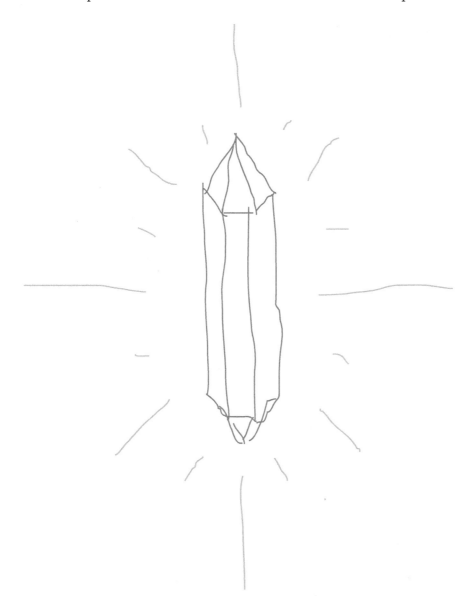

In this way, deadname communicated five ideas to Strawberry-Witch. They are as follows:

1. You hold thousands of monsters inside your body.
2. You are a segment of time, rather than space & most of the confusion you have experienced throughout your life is the result of a misconception about this.
3. When Dog-Witch created the world, ze did not plan delicately, but did so by instinct. By muscle memory.
4. How many times can a person think about bashing their own head open before trying it. I'm scared. How many times can anyone even do this.
5. Someone please help.

Strawberry-Witch especially understood these last two points. When she was alone sometimes she would imagine destruction on a grand scale. There was a way in which this sort of thought was incredibly comforting. She would cry when she thought of this, always these big, messy cries where she was stringing snot & spit all over the front of her romper. She decided that some day she would start a religion that worshipped a meteor, praying for it to come to earth & crush everything. She never started this religion but it came to exist anyway. Some things are inevitable.

Strawberry-Witch had the dream about being inside the bird's stomach again but this time the bird was vomiting. It was trying to expel her but it wasn't working. The walls constricted, pressing on her body, hard. She even tried to help it get her out, but there was nothing to be done.

This is volume one of Sea-Witch. There is more where this came from. The text of this book was originally published at the Sea-Witch patreon. You can subscribe to read the text of future volumes of Sea-Witch before they are put into print at http://patreon.com/monstr.

ABOUT THE AUTHOR
Moss Angel Witchmonstr is a scorpio because of fucking course she is.
Find her online at http://moonbears.biz

HI THANKS

Thanks to Irene Milsom & Prairie M Faul for being my first readers & family. Thanks to Colette Arrand for publishing a bunch of this & believing in this project. Thanks to joseph parker okay and Elijah Pearson for making this book happen & being amazing editors. Thanks to Jordaan Mason for being such an inspiration always. Thanks to Nikki Wallschlaeger, Precious Okoyomon, Blake Butler & Raquel Salas Rivera for contributing blurbs to this project. Thanks to Chaya Romanova for being my Sea-Witch. Thanks to Echo Darwin, Hazel Grace Evergreen, JoeyJane Marie Lovechild, Jade Eklund, Lucy Wood & others who have been there for me emotionally & spiritually. Thanks to all the subscribers to the Sea-Witch patreon. Thanks to all the queer & trans monstrs in the pacific northwest who supported me so hard when the cis lit world stopped giving a shit. Love to all the families of those slain by cops. Love to those resisting at Standing Rock & around the world. Love to those who have been crushed by the weight of capitalism. Love to my fellow monstrs: the trans women, the mentally ill, the sex workers. This one is for you. Love to all the other monsters who suffer things I don't have to: even though deserve is one of the words that doesn't make sense in Sea-Witch, you deserve the world. Love & solidarity to the anticapitalists out there fighting against this fucked up system of prisons & borders & laws & cops.

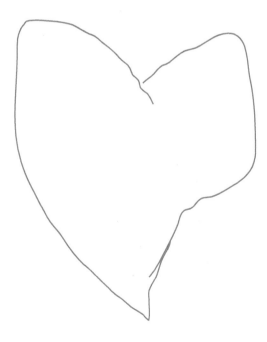

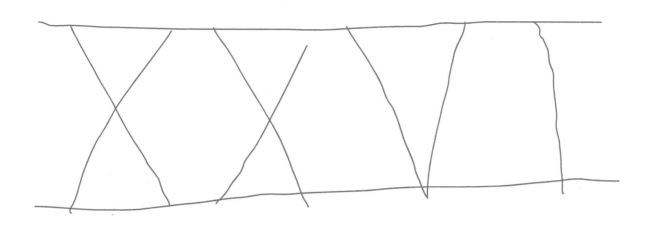

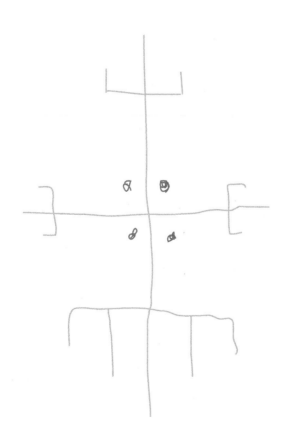

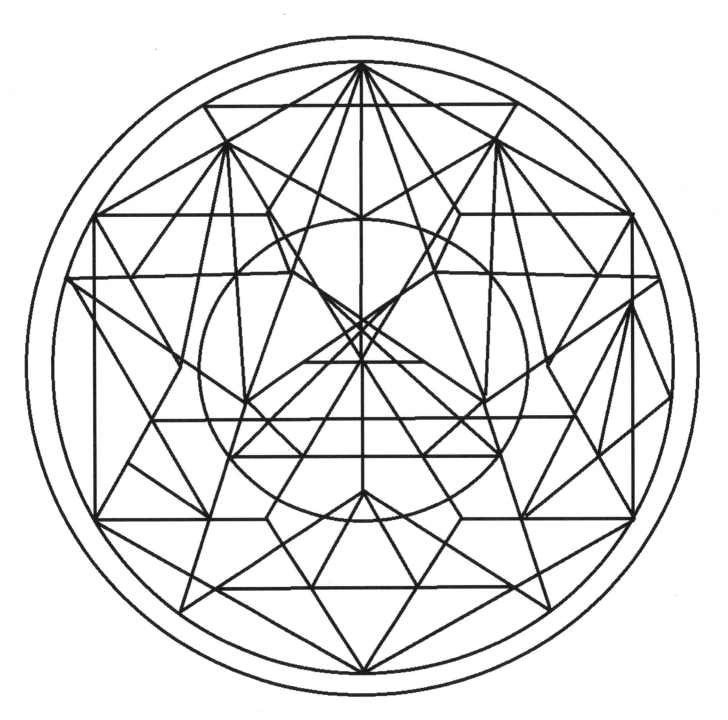

sigil of peace, ending capitalism, healing trauma, and hot trans makeouts by claire diane